PU]

Mathias Hardeman, Sr.

CONTENTS

Introduction

This book is written to expose a church that elicits wrongful acts among its congregation: The House of Prayer in Atlanta, Georgia.

I was born and raised in this church by both of my parents. When I became a young teenager, I was forced to accept the theological teachings and crafty measures of Reverend Arthur Allen, Jr. I did not understand what Reverend Allen knew all along, as I was young and vulnerable. It was easy for Reverend Allen to develop the church as a cult as generations came along. New generations of children such as myself—growing up under cunning, deceitful, and domineering proceedings used for personal gain—gave him the power to control and manipulate people into submission.

After many years, I fought back against the unconventional and harmful teachings that Reverend Allen instilled in my mind. On January 1, 2012, I left the church because of Reverend Allen's dishonest actions. I was afraid as I planned my exit, because I knew that I would lose not only my family and friends, but my loved ones would devalue my character and shun me.

Throughout this book, Reverend Arthur Allen is referred to as "Reverend Allen" and/or "pastor."

It is my hope that this book will help readers recognize the characteristics of a cult-led foundation. Because I was once part of a church cult, I can share my story of bondage.

What Is a Cult?

A specific system of religious worship, especially with reference to its rites and deity. A religious organization using devious psychological techniques to gain and control adherents. An intense interest in and devotion to a person, idea, activity, or something regarded as fashionable or significant by a particular group or relating to or characterized by a cult figure.

Collins English Dictionary - Complete & Unabridged 10th Edition 2009 © William Collins Sons & Co. Ltd. 1979, 1986 © HarperCollins Publishers 1998, 2000, 2003, 2005, 2006, 2007, 2009

In the 1930s, cults were studied in the context of religious belief and behavior. They have been criticized by mainstream Christians for their unorthodox beliefs. Every cult has a single, powerful leader who proclaims that he is God on earth. Do you recall Jim Jones or Charles Manson? They both claimed to be Jesus Christ. In the 1970s, the anti-cult movement arose, motivated partly by the violence committed by groups such as the Manson Family and the People's Temple.

Cults seem wonderful on the outside but are manipulative on the inside. Cult leaders are desperate to trick members into joining. They are after the members' obedience, time, and money. The sophisticated mind-control and recruitment techniques that they use are refined over time. Beware of thinking that you are immune. Millions of cult members around the world once thought they were immune and still do not know they are in a cult! To recognize a cult, you need to know how they work and understand the crafty techniques they use.

Cult leaders want to be feared—to disagree with them is the same as disagreeing with God.

The leaders will claim to have authority from God to control almost all aspects of your life. Questioning the leader or program will be seen as a sign of rebellion and stupidity. They will use guilt to control you. For example, a leader might say, "Maybe you're not making money because you're not with our program. Maybe you're not able to convert new recruits because your heart is prideful and full of sin. Maybe you are enduring sickness because of a sin or wrongful act you have committed in your past life and God is punishing you." It could never be that the program isn't working or that the new recruits have valid reasons for not joining. It's always your fault, you are always wrong, and you must try harder!

If you disobey any written or unwritten rules, the cult members will use character assassination to make you feel guilty.

The core of a cult is control. An innumerable amount of people, whether former members or supporters, are not fully aware of the extent to which other members may have been manipulated, exploited, or abused.

The House of Prayer

Reverend Arthur Allen, Jr. founded the House of Prayer church in 1966. The nondenominational congregation has approximately 200 members. The church began meeting in the homes of congregational members. They eventually purchased a building located at 1194 Hollywood Road in northwest Atlanta.

The House of Prayer came under fire in 2001 for allegations of cruelty to children inside their local Atlanta church. One child, according to a police officer was beaten so severely it appeared to be an imprint of a belt buckle on his body. It was reported that two boys had bruises, abrasions and scars on their bodies after receiving a beating with a switch and a belt by members of the church. The House of Prayer made headline news. Several networks, stations and people got involved which included but not limited to Dateline NBC, CNN, Fox News, AJC, BBC, People Magazine, Bryant Gumbel, Bill O'Reilly, Sally Jessy Raphael and Nancy Grace.

The Rev. Arthur Allen and five other people were arrested. Forty-one children were removed from their families and put in foster care amid allegations that Allen directed members of the congregation of his Atlanta church (the House of Prayer) to beat their children. The pastor said that the bible teaches that it is right to punish children by beating them, so they will learn how wrong it is to misbehave.

The children would be taken to the church for discipline, which would be organized by the pastor. In most instances, three or four adults would hold them with arms and legs suspended in an airborne position while two or three others would beat them until the pastor said to stop.

The pastor was eventually convicted of cruelty to children which he served two consecutive years in prison and eight years on probation. The pastor has never attended any theological seminaries and has only a high school education. Reverend Allen insists that he listens only to God's voice. Flaunting himself continuously, he eludes to having special powers God has granted to him through the holy spiritual realm.

Some beliefs he conveys to his followers are:

•Reverend Allen announces that he does not have examples of any apostles in the Bible going to seminary. Allen believes that God gave him the authority to interpret Scripture and that he is the only one that has the knowledge to know how to lead the House of Prayer church. He often replies "I don't report to anyone under myself."

•The pastor forbids the members to ever challenge him on anything. "Challenging me," he says, "is as if you are challenging God."

•Reverend Allen believes that the House of Prayer is the only church that he is aware of that really "knows God."

•The pastor has a disdain for law.
•It is trendy for the pastor to kidnap children that has been awarded by the court to the parent that has left his church.

•The pastor preaches that the forbidden fruit that is spoken of in the King James Version of the bible concerning Adam and Eve was oral sex.

•The pastor does not allow members to marry anyone outside of the church.

•The exact same day the pastor's second wife of forty-three years was buried; he went off and married a twenty-three year old woman at his age of sixty- eight years old.

•Reverend Allen coerces female children to marry at very early ages to men significantly older.

•The pastor encourages children to dishonor and disrespect parents that are no longer part of his church.

•Reverend Allen strongly uses perverse, derogatory, vulgar and degrading language in front of small children during church services.

Mind Control and Deception

Mind control is a suite of psychological techniques that cult leaders use to control members. It does not turn people into "remote-control robots" (it is not some sort of irresistible force like aliens

used in movies). It is more like a psychological "gun." The leader points the mind-control "gun" at a member and says, "If you leave us, you will lose all your friends and family," or "If you don't conform, you will go to hell," or "If you don't give us money, you will fail in business."
A cult needs to recruit and operate using deception (if people knew the true practices and beliefs beforehand, they would not join).

A cult will have a slick, well-rehearsed front that hides what the group is really like. You will hear how it helps the poor or supports research, peace, or the environment. Leaders will tell you how happy you will be, and everyone in the cult will always seem happy and enthusiastic (they have been told to act happy and will be punished if they don't).

You will not be told what life is really like in the group or what it really believes. These will be introduced to you slowly. You will not notice the changes until you realize that you are practicing and believing things that, at the start, would have caused you to run.

A normal religious organization does not have any trouble with people moving to a similar organization as long as they stay in that same religion. It is generally the belief system that matters, not membership in a specific organization. For example, if you are a Christian, you can move from one church to another and "still be a Christian." However, a cult leader will tell you that you can be "saved" or be "successful" only in his organization. No other organization has the truth; all others miss the mark. It is not the belief system that decides your future, but the belief system and your membership with the group.

Cult leaders make you believe that if you ever leave the "one true church," you are going to hell. This fear-based mechanism is designed to keep you trapped in the cult. It gives the leaders tremendous power over you. If you really believe that leaving the group equals leaving God or leaving your only chance to succeed in life, you obey the cult leaders even when you disagree with them. You don't want to risk being kicked out.

Candidate for Membership

You must be willing to denounce all your family members—mother, father, sister, and brother—to prove that you are worthy of The House of Prayer church.

If any of your relatives are not a part of this church, you are told to separate yourself from them. For example, if your mother had a child out of wedlock, confronting her and telling her that she is a whore and a slut affirms your acceptance. If your father was a womanizer, he must be confronted and called names such as whoremonger or whorehead. All the members of your family must be confronted in the same manner. You will be given Bible scriptures that support these actions, such as Luke 14:26 and Matthew 8:22. Mark 3:33 states, "Who is my mother and my brother?"

You will be encouraged to stand up in front of the congregation to say that you have officially disowned all family members outside the church. This proves your loyalty to the church, and the congregation will accept you as a member with rousing applause. You must then cut off your ties with everyone who is not related to you by blood: childhood friends, old classmates, or other people you know.

Service to the group is put before your own life, and members continuously praise your actions as "grounded in God" and in his approval. The pastor would then use high-pressure tactics to get people to join the church and extreme measures to make them stay. He knew that the convert's loved ones would eventually reveal the group's evil agenda.

Brainwashing

The pastor preached long, annoying sermons that included shouting and a lengthy vulgar conversation about sex. He rarely opened the bible because speaking of all types of sex acts was his favorite subject in church. Additionally, we were told to constantly repeat that we were dumb, no good, stupid, doomed for failure and a trashy nigger bound for hell if we ever left the church. He often said that we were "slow-minded dummies" if we didn't do things exactly the way he thought was necessary.

Reverend Allen made us (the members) feel like we were empty headed and needed a dictator like him to do our thinking for us, and as long as he did, we would fare well in life. He constantly reminded us that out of all the churches, he related his church to the characteristics of the "church of Smyrna" as it is referred to in the Book of Revelation located in the King James Bible. In Revelation 2:8, God expressed he was pleased with the "church of Smyrna" and the way they worshipped him. Allen would have all members to constantly chant amen and right after everything he says for many long hours.

He would deprive us from sleep and tell us to stand against the wall if we were sleepy. He said we are not going to be sleeping on him while he is expounding on the words of God. He said at least if we stood against the wall while sleepy and fall onto the hard concrete floor and hit our heads, he would be satisfied.

Many times services would be held well into the following day. Those of us who held on the clock jobs could not leave for work without his direct permission. In many instances we would raise our hands like little children and ask to be excused from service. He would tell us, "No God comes before our jobs and to call in to tell our bosses we're not coming in at all that day." Some of us would even sacrifice our jobs or give up our livelihood if it meant putting Allen on the back burner or putting our jobs before him.

He constantly reminded us that we were a bunch of nobodies who would never be nothing without him. And in our eyes, he was the only somebody out of the entire church.

Openly Rebuked, Scorned, and Shamed

The pastor ordered you to come before the church and tell your darkest secrets whether they revealed homosexuality, womanizing, drug addiction, suicide attempts, or sexual addiction. After confessing your sins, he probed into your life as if he were trying to help you recover. He convinced you to "let go" of your most shameful secrets and made you feel comfortable (while he used others as bait to befriend you).

He later rehashed your secrets and used your confession to hurt you; constantly calling you the names that you offered in your confession. He tried to make you think that you were not worthy of love, butchering your self-esteem. Many members ended up feeling that the only person worthy of God's love was Reverend Allen. Additionally, he would hold over your head for years the confessions you made openly about your shameful past.

If you ever decided to go against him for any of his wrong doings, he'll remind the members of your old characteristics or lifestyle to silence you. That way in the sight of others, you would lose credibility as to the complaints that you have against him.

He would say you are the drug addict, liar, sex addict, etc... His demeaning comments trigger the members to shout at you speaking words of destruction. They would call names and say, "liar," or "you are the sinner" or scream "the Devil is using you to attack and destroy our pastor." You then decide to give in and apologize to Allen in tears because it is too many of them against you to fight off alone.

Control Every Aspect of Life

At the age 15, I was groomed for life in the cult without being aware of it. Reverend Allen had finally caught up with me and found a reason to abuse me, too. He ordered 4 adult men in the church to suspend me in the air by both my hands and legs while the 5th man beat me with a belt. After the beating was over, he gave me $100.00 to spend, attempting to buy my affection towards him. The pastor explained how I was "just like a son to him" and how I impacted his life. He had an evil and conniving way of breaking you down inwardly and building you back up emotionally, for you to reverence him in the end.

He later had the church to buy me my first car after I turned sixteen; the church bought it for me because the pastor said I was good natured and he liked me. This was his way of rewarding me. Reverend Allen advised me to confide in him, but not make any major decisions without consulting him first. As time passed, the pastor ended up forcing me against my wishes to get married at the age of seventeen to a young girl in the church. All I could do is cry because I felt my life was being taken from me at a young age.

The pastor encouraged me to drop out of school and have as many children as possible with my new wife. This was his way of growing his congregation from the inside out because he always wanted a mega church. One of his greatest quotes from the bible was "be fruitful and multiply." You were told who to marry. Teenagers were taken across the state line to marry at age fourteen, because it was forbidden in Georgia. Girls were coerced into marrying significantly older men.

Reverend Allen believed that he had authority over your wife and was the man of your house. He encouraged women to come to him if their husbands tried to make decisions about their household. The men of the church were not in charge of their own houses. We were totally emasculated.

We couldn't buy a house, car or go on a vacation without first consulting him and getting his permission. Decisions about careers or finances had to meet his approval. The pastor mandated that in order for God to bless our decisions, he had to personally sign it first.

Reverend Allen always mentioned that God granted him special powers. He said that only he could hear God's voice and give direction to his congregation because he was just like Jesus. He expressed feeling that he was born of God and filled with the Holy Ghost, and his members were like "little children" to him. The pastor reminded us if we challenged him on anything, we were challenging God.

No Socialization with the Outside World

Reverend Allen encouraged every member of the church to live in or near his compound; outsiders were not permitted. He wanted all social activities to "stay within the confines of the church." If the pastor found out that you patronized anyone outside the church, he came against you.

For example, when one man and his wife went outside the church to get a haircut, they were told that they displayed a selfish behavior and should have patronized someone in the church. If you needed a barber, realtor, mechanic, or other professionals, you were told to be a customer only to the people in the church.

He held services that sometimes lasted a whole day. Children were held in church for long hours. Other days that were set aside for recreational hours, only meant we would attend church five days a week after Reverend Allen stepped onto his soap box to ruin recreational fun time.

Eventually, the pastor ordered all members to remove their children from public schools. Reverend Allen stated that if the congregation ever beat the children again and left marks on them, the state would not find out. Therefore, he suggested for all children to be homeschooled.

Most of the children, including my own, who were homeschooled could barely read or write at the standard grade level. Most of the teachers were mothers who didn't even have a high school education and were not adequately prepared to teach children. With all the long, drawn-out services, parents had little time to teach their own children. The children enrolled in testing, could not pass the tests mandated by the state for homeschooled students.

The pastor did not promote careers. If you were self-sufficient, it threatened his ability to control your life. He resented the fact that I went back to finish school without his blessing and eventually earned a professional business of my own.

Degradation

Reverend Allen had women and men announce in front of the church how big their vaginas were and had the men measure their penises in front of the children. He often referenced to male genitals to describe the women vaginas implying that their vaginal area was similar to "big cocks" and continued taunting them by saying they have "big sloppy pussies" and that no one wanted them before they came to the church. The pastor told them, in front of their husbands, how fat and ugly they were and how they needed to lose weight. The husbands would agree with him that he had the authority to talk to their wives that way. One man made the comment that his wife "had a big sloppy pussy," he had a little penis, and they are not sexually compatible. Reverend Allen said that if they were not in his church, they wouldn't be able to resolve their problem.

One man was crippled from childhood, and the pastor told him that no woman had wanted him before he entered into the church. He used demeaning phrases, saying "no one wanted your wife because she was a whore and a slut" and that no one outside the church would be attracted to her. The pastor said, "Most of you before joining this church were no good, pussy lickers, dick suckers, cock suckers, whores, whoremongers, sluts, and niggers."

He knew how to damage your self-esteem and hold things against you. He told members, "This church is your savior and staying here is the only way to avoid being stigmatized."

Adultery

While he was married to his second wife, Rev. Allen had sex with a teenage girl in the church while preaching strongly about God being against those who commit adultery and live in sin. The pastor had been having sex with her in various locations. He didn't care whether it was in the back seat of a station wagon car or outside in the woods on the ground.

At least on one occasion, the pastor was having sex with her in the basement of his wife's house. His wife heard them through the floor, but was too afraid to confront him. Reverend Allen had a reputation of cowardly physically beating his wife after they had heated arguments.

Subsequently, his wife stumbled upon used condoms under their house and finally gathered the nerve to ask him about it. He lied and indicated that he didn't know how the condoms got there. He later got caught red handed having sex with her again at the girl's house by her sister. Finally, the pastor felt that he could no longer lie about his molestation and adultery.

After a long confession of his wretched acts, he still continued having sex with her for years afterwards. He had stolen her virginity and left her feeling robbed, abused and emotionally distraught. She eventually left the church after becoming an adult, feeling that he had no regards, respect or care for her at all.

The pastor relentlessly preached against adultery and sin while molesting other young girls as well. He also continued committing adultery with several women inside and outside of the church. Additionally, his wife had no real value to him. She would sometimes tell him about his womanizing behavior and how she could not preserve the way he treated their marriage. Rev. Allen would then start to abuse her and tell her if she's going to cry and complain about it, she should go into another room. That way he said he didn't have to see her face.

Reverend Allen really abused her not only physically but emotionally as well for many years. She later got sick with cancer and he advised her not to go to the hospital for treatment. He waited until the cancer had taken over her body and then recommended for her to seek medical help.

By the time the doctors tried to help her it was too late and she died shortly thereafter. I perceived him wanting her to die because he had already began making sexual advances towards another young woman around 50 years his junior in the church.

Fear

On several occasions, I heard Reverend Allen boast about how he used to rape women when they wouldn't give him sex. The pastor tricked women into performing oral sex on him. He grabbed their heads and ejaculated in their mouths as they tried to pull away. Occasionally he had sex with men and boasted about having sex with more than one hundred women. "If you broke God's commandments and continue to break them, God will allow you to become ill as punishment for your sins," he would exclaim.

Reverend Allen told one man, "If you play with God, our savior will allow a stroke to hit you." Not long after the pastor spoke these words, he himself became not only the victim of a stroke, but according to his physician, he possibly incurred two or three heart attacks during the progression of his stroke.

To keep the members living in fear, he talked about people who left the church and became alcoholics or prostitutes. You had to do what you were told at all times. If he told you to sit somewhere, you said nothing and simply obeyed. Challenging him on anything was forbidden. He knew how to use your best friend, mother, father, sister, brother, wife, or husband against you. Allen used them to badger you and side with him even if he was wrong, knowing that it would be hard to withstand him.

During one sermon, the pastor made the comment that in the bible, Peter who was a Jew pulled away from preaching to the Gentiles because of fear of losing the influence he had on them. At that time, the

Gentiles were considered to be unclean to the Jews. Reverend Allen said that Apostle Paul corrected Peter but not according to knowledge but because he didn't have the authority to make Peter preach to the Gentiles. This made no sense to me. If Paul corrected Peter but it wasn't according to knowledge, what did he correct him by? I was always taught that in order to correct a wrong, you must use knowledge to do so.

I tried to question the pastor on his interpretation. The pastor turned to me and said that I had a snake and a devil in me for questioning him, which to this day does not make sense to me. Then again, how do you make sense out of something that makes no sense?

Reverend Allen told me that he hated me and had my biological brother and others to tell me to my face that they all hate me as well. He told me that I didn't belong at his church. His words were, "Maybe you belong at Eddie Long's church;

he seems to like young men." This was said to make mockery and belittle me. I also knew what my brother said was not true because he was only being used as a puppet. Prior to my brother telling me this, he mentioned to me that he did not think the pastor liked him. He also stated that different members in the church were peace breakers. He was left feeling the pastor had abused his authority in a matter concerning his family.

I knew he didn't have the courage to say this to the pastor because he was afraid of his wrath. This was enough to make me surrender and stop any thoughts of being at odds or in disagreement with my brother. It pained me to see my brother between a rock and a hard place. I knew we were very close from childhood and that we deeply loved one another.

Sex

The pastor said that he was a "superman in the bedroom" despite the fact that he was eighty years of age. His wife was substantially younger than him, and the pastor boasted about how he could handle her sexually. Reverend Allen felt a sense of accomplishment and pride because he plummeted her thirties in age.

According to the pastor's confession, he found it difficult to have an erection when his wife was in the heat of passion one night. He realized that his "mojo" was slipping away and could not perform sexually to please his wife. He shoved a banana into her vagina. She immediately told him how he disrespected and degraded her and that she would bring his actions out in front of the church.

Eventually, she did. His wife blurted out in front of the members his violation towards her, how he sinned against her, and made her feel like she was a cheap and loose woman. Nervously, she asked the women of the church how they would feel if their husbands shoved a banana in their vagina.

Reverend Allen told his wife not to challenge him; that he was the man and the pastor. He said that God had granted him power over her and that he was the one who "bailed her out" when her ex-husband ran off and left her with five children. He ranted on and on about helping her when she didn't have anything and the financial independence he had given her.

During the next service, he retaliated. He might have felt that people would no longer see him as a "superman" because of the way he had treated his wife in the bedroom, even though he encouraged members to "bring out their disparities and sinful nature" in church.

The service lasted until seven in the morning and his wife fell asleep. He told her to wake up, stand against the wall, and not fall asleep or go into to the back room. The pastor said it was repulsive to fall asleep while he was preaching. When she refused to get up, he grabbed her cellphone, broke it up with his hands and threw it on the floor. The Reverend yelled, "I destroyed your phone because I mean business. When I tell you to do something, you do it right away." He told her that if she did not stay awake, he would have men haul her to the back room and her children would see her kicking and screaming while the men dragged her through the halls. The pastor was a ruthless being; degrading his wife in front of everybody like she was trash and was pouring salt on her wound.

It was very common for Allen to discuss sex in church. This is how he got his jollies. For hours at a time he would always tell how it was commonplace for him to have sex with women with big sloppy pussies. He said he wanted to experience a tighter pussy which is why he claims he married his first wife. He said that she told him that she was a virgin and wasn't having sex until marriage and he thought his ship had come in. Whether it's true or not the pastor would always say that he was madly disappointed again.

The pastor would then talk about his current wife in front of her face of how sloppy her pussy is as well. He would ask us do our wives have a tight pussy or a sloppy pussy. We would have to shout whether it is tight or sloppy. Then he would talk to us about how big or little our dicks are in the church. These are his words, not mine. He would go on for hours talking about our sex lives in our bedroom. Next he would ask who ever ate pussy before. Then he would ask who has ever sucked dicks before. The men and the woman would take turns telling sexual graphic details of how it is to do oral sex, anal sex and even sex with animals. All of this in the presence of minor children.

Loyalty

Reverend Allen gave impoverished people thousands of dollars to renovate their dilapidated houses, and by doing so, he bought their affection. Some people received cars so that they would feel indebted to him.

He rented rat- and roach-infested houses that were "a step up" for most of his members. The members believed that Reverend Allen was doing them a special favor. Most of them had been raised in some of the worst projects in Atlanta; some were homeless, hustlers, gangbangers, prostitutes, and suicidal. Through his actions, the pastor gained influence with them.

Additionally, many of us would give the pastor our right arm or pluck out our eyeballs for him if he requested them. We would go through great heights to show him our loyalty. Many times we would risk our own lives for him. That means come hell or high water or even illegal activities, we would lay down our lives for him. We would even betray our own blood relatives to prove our allegiance to him.

Praised as Jesus

During lessons or his long rituals, Reverend Allen often referred to the Bible verse that says, "Let the greatest among you be your servant." He asked, "Who is the greatest in this church?" The members replied in unison, "You are." In response to everything he said, whether right or wrong, the members chanted "Amen" repeatedly and nodded their heads in agreement. The members persistently declared that they had "never met a man like him" and that Jesus was "in him."

Reverend Allen often said that the world did not know him because people didn't know Jesus. He told his third wife, who was forty-five years younger than him, to confess a dream that she had about him. In the dream, he died, and she turned his body over. His backside was branded with the name JESUS.

He often said that he felt as if he had powers that others did not and that he was not a normal man but some type of spiritual being. He relished this, and the members upheld his delusion. He would tell us just like Jesus is the Lord of heaven, he is the Lord of the earth.

Beating Wives into Submission

When I was a young boy, I wondered why my dad once had my mom down on her knees and beat her badly with a belt. I wanted to stop him but didn't know how. This developed an ache and anger throughout my life that lasted for years, and I could not do anything but cry. I remember saying to myself that when I get grown, I will never let him beat my mom again.

As I grew older, I learned that he was influenced by the pastor to beat my mom with a belt because she had once left the church and tried to get away. Then I heard two other men in the church laugh and boast about how Allen told them to beat their wives constantly with a belt until they submitted to them.

Even after marrying at such an early age, my wife and I began to have marital trouble. The pastor told me that when my wife rebelled against me, I should take her freedom away. He said, "Take all of her money, the keys to her car and disconnect the battery, take her cellphone, cut off all connection, and don't give it back until I say so. This is called the good fight of faith and she will fully surrender and submit to you."

I followed his orders, cutting off all of her luxuries, stripping her to the bare minimum for survival. I felt guilty over this even though the pastor told me that God approved. Eventually, I returned everything that I had taken from her. When the pastor found out, he scorned me in front of the church, yelling that I was "nothing but a hen-pecked coward" and that I should have consulted him first. This is how he instructed all the men concerning their wives.

One woman testified that when she was nine months pregnant, the pastor advised her husband to beat her with a belt. He read scriptures that proclaimed how women are saved through child bearing and that obedience to their husband is recognized by God. If they submitted to their husbands and continued in faith, which means to reside in the House of Prayer.

Cruelty to Adults and Children

The pastor had children who he felt were misbehaving come before the church and ordered four men to suspend them in the air. A fifth person would be ordered to beat the child. He told them to beat the child until he or she surrendered.

I witnessed a child being suspended in the air by four men and the pastor ordering him to be beaten. He was beaten until his skin peeled off of his back. Reverend Allen praised the beater. He told the men how long a child should be beaten and when to stop. After many children were beaten, the pastor praised the man who gave the children the hardest blow with a belt. Afterwards, the pastor and members laughed. Reverend Allen boasted, "This man sure knows how to beat those children."

From time to time, I saw the pastor commanding grown men to be whipped. He said that they were stubborn and quoted from the bible, "It takes a rod for a fool's back."

I witnessed on another account as a child, the pastor arranging for a married woman to be severely beaten with a belt. He instructed the men and her mother to hold her down and abuse her. He said that she was trying to poison the minds of the other young girls to not marry so young. The pastor taunted her saying, "beat her until she cries. You're going to cry, give in and submit." He allowed her to be beaten until she nearly passed out. She could barely breathe because she suffered from asthma.

Her spineless husband stood by and did nothing to rescue his wife. This made me angry, and I felt helpless. I knew it was wrong and inhumane. Even as an adult, I witnessed a married women that was about 7 or 8 months pregnant get beaten with a belt because the pastor didn't like the way she spoke to him. This behavior show insanity; even animals get treated better.

Hazing

Because I wanted to be a minister, I conducted lessons in the church. The pastor noticed my talent and felt that I was trying to "steal his thunder." He wanted the members to idolize him. When he saw that I was gaining influence over some members and would try and correct some of his evil and foul teachings, he encouraged them to mistreat me in atrocious and unyielding ways. He undoubtedly compelled the members to label me:

- Self-centered
- Inferior (my way of teaching didn't match his)
- Unskilled (God didn't give me the talent to minister only the pastor presumably received that from God)

- Condemned (I had not been "anointed" like the pastor had)

They insulted and belittled me for years to discourage me from conducting lessons in the church ever again. Some members enjoyed the lessons I conducted more than they enjoyed Reverend Allen's. I had become the director of two choirs. When I did not go along with the pastor on his wrong doings, he began to take privileges away from me. He banned me from being the choir director. He allowed the members in the church to taunt and scorn me openly for many years. They butchered my self-esteem and made me feel worthless. When other members did not go along with the pastor, they were ostracized also.

On one occasion, I can recall Reverend Allen calling a girl to the front of the church after she got into mischief, cutting her sister's hair while her sister was asleep. The pastor ordered her father to get some scissors and cut off the girl's hair. The girl's mother complained about it, but to no avail.

The same woman's oldest daughter made a confession in the church and to the pastor. She did not want her confession broadcasted that her mother had been on the Internet chatting romantically with another man outside of her marriage. Reverend Allen confronted the mother about it in front of the church, but the mother declined to discuss it, saying that she would rather leave the church. The pastor influenced the mother's husband to take all of her money and not to allow any of the mother's children to go with her, cut off the electricity in her house, and have the water turned off.

Designated members of the church searched the mother's purse and did not allow her to leave until they stripped her of all her valuables. I thought that even if the girl's confession about her mother was true, there is a right way and a wrong way to deal with it. First of all, she shouldn't have been forced to marry him being much older than her when she was only 14 years of age. That within itself makes no sense to me.

Disdain for Law

The Bible says, "The law is good if a man uses it lawfully." Reverend Allen often referred to the verse, "The law was not made for a righteous man but for the lawless, murderers, thieves, manslayers." Because the pastor thought he was a "so-called righteous man," "filled with the spirit of Jesus," he did not have to abide by laws.

The pastor bought rental properties or houses and remodeled them without a permit and had a tricky way of doing it. He advised landscapers to dump truck loads of trash on other people's property. He figured out conniving ways to build without permits. For example, he illegally ran power wires from one house to the next. He tapped into underground pipes to get around building codes and permits in ways that could not be discovered.

After the pastor was convicted of cruelty to children in 2001, he served two years in prison. He was told by a superior court judge in Fulton County to never partake in beatings where children were suspended in the air and whipped. After his release from jail, he continued with the same practices and I witnessed them.

From time to time, members pulled away from the church, and some had to fight for custody of their children. After one man left the church and got custody of his children, the pastor kidnapped the children and had them taken to another state before the man could retrieve them. I saw this happen with other parents, also.

Occasionally, the pastor hid children in the houses of various church members. When authorities asked about the children's whereabouts, the pastor always denied having knowledge of it. Later, children might be found in Mexico or other places after been located by the authorities.

Relatives Marrying

Although the United States has laws against relatives marrying, it is believed these laws are driven to eliminate the ability of reproduction. Reverend Allen claimed he asked God if he (the pastor) should allow relatives to marry. He felt that though the law may not approve, if God gave him insight, then God had condoned the marriages. This is because he doesn't allow his members to date or marry anyone outside of his cult. It forces him then to start looking on the inside of marrying blood relatives because again he's trying to grow his church. The pastor said that he could care less what the law enforced as long as he received a direct message from God. Many of the marriages that Reverend Allen supported were between teenage girls and men who were older by ten years or more.

Molestation

One young church member came to her father and told him that a man in the church had molested her. The father told the pastor what happened. The pastor confronted the man, and the man said that the accusation was false. This caused the other members to be suspicious of him. When he could no longer hide his lies, he admitted to fondling children from the age of nine months to seven years old.

More children began to come forward to acknowledge how he had abused them. One boy said before the church and his parents that the man forced him and his young brother to suck his penis. This caused an uproar in the church. The man gave the graphic details of how he molested innocent babies, sometimes carrying out sick, perverse practices in church. He said that while he held a girl, around twenty-four months old, he put his finger in her vagina. He described in detail how when the other member's heads were bowed during the benediction, he held the little girl and looked over at the girl's mother. Next, he put his hand over the girl's mouth while his finger was in her vagina because the little girl screamed that it hurt.

When he named some of the girls and boys he had molested, I heard the name of one of my daughters. I questioned my daughter immediately. The man then walked up to me and admitted to my face that he molested my daughter. He began giving graphic details of how he preyed upon her. I nearly lost it.

The members of the church questioned the child molester. The pastor told us to stop questioning him and leave him alone because we didn't know how to deal with him. I wanted to slaughter the man for what he had done not only to my child, but to other innocent children. If I ever felt there was a time to kill, that was it.

Reverend Allen advised all members not to report the molester to the authorities because he was going to deal with the matter himself. Reverend Allen advised the molester to marry a young woman and said to him "since you seem to be fascinated with young girl's pussies, now you can experience an adult pussy."

When I found out about the molestation of the children and that the pastor had influenced many men including my dad to beat their wives with belts and abuse them while allowing the molester in the church to walk around free, it was a pivotal point for me. I saw how heartless he was and the brutality he advised. Finally, my eyes were beginning to open.

The pastor did nothing to deal with the issue, so I left the church and had the child molester prosecuted by the authorities. I realized that the pastor did not do anything because he was a child molester himself.

Excommunication

Throughout the years, I observed such practices going on in the church. I witnessed how the pastor alienated, ostracized, and "excommunicated" people from their siblings, children, the friends that they grew up with, and their loved ones, including their own parents. I saw Reverend Allen kidnap children because a parent might decide that he or she wants to leave the church. I saw children hidden under church pews, in classrooms, in the woods outside the church, taken across state lines, and hidden from authorities.

I recall the struggle of a man who had pulled away from the church and gained sole custody of his children. The pastor kidnapped the children and would not turn them over to the man. The authorities got involved and questioned the pastor, who said that he did not know where the children were (even though he paid to hide them). The pastor deprived the cult members of those who were dearest to them and needed them the most.

Witnessing how the pastor had people degrade a member who wanted to leave the church was mind-boggling. Your family would tell you that you are doomed to hell and you would become a low-life, trashy, a whore, a whoremonger, a slut, and a nigger. All of this was combined with a disdain for the law, hazing, degradation, molestation, and cruelty. I witnessed all of this with my own eyes.

If you left the church, it was believed that you left God. You were considered an outcast. You lost all your family and friends. Everything you had gained or had worked for was snatched away. I had lost faith in God because of the trauma I received in my life. I felt like if God was real, he would have never allowed me to suffer this type of pain in my life from birth. I asked the question many times, what is my purpose for being in this world? I felt that if life offers no more than what I have experienced in this cult, I'd rather be dead. I became hopeless and no longer wanted to live.

I finally realized that the man I was taught to worship, idolize, honor, praise, glorify and reverence was no more than a Pulpit Gangster.

My Escape

The retribution that I had seen happen to others happened to me. I lost my wife, mother, father, sisters, brothers, and childhood friends. I knew that I had to be willing to lose them all in order to get away.

I tried many times to rescue my wife. I took her on a vacation in hope to help her understand why we should leave the church. After inviting her to go to marriage counseling, I spent many hours pleading, trying to convince her that the church was not the place for our family. It was destroying us and our family. I stressed the importance of rescuing ourselves and our nine children.

The pastor later told my wife and all 9 of my young children to call me degrading, belittling names to my face when they got home from church. My wife did as he instructed, encouraging my oldest son down to my 2 year old to take turns calling me names.

They repeatedly called me dumb, stupid, liar, trash, nigger and dog. She yelled at me and said, "Every day you step foot in this house, it's going to be war nigger!" Furthermore, they started throwing my clothes and shoes at me shouting, "Bye trash, we want you out of the house." This really hurt me deeply to see my children being used in such an odious and egregious way towards me. I became even more determined to rescue my children from this abusive cult. My wife eventually made her final decision. She decided to be true and loyal to the pastor and no longer wanted to be married to me because I left the church.

Several days after leaving the church, I called my father. I told him that I did not agree with the pastor and could not find scriptures in the Bible that supported his activities. He told me that God dealt with the pastor directly and that even if I didn't find scripture verses that supported his practices, whatever the pastor said, I should "shut up, sit down, and take it."

My father told me that he should have whipped me more when I was younger. If he had, maybe I would not have left the church. He said that until I returned to the church, he doesn't need a son like me and he doesn't need a phone call from me ever again. I later talked to several people that advised me to never give up on God. They said that there is still life worth living outside of this church and to never allow anyone to tell me different. They told me God is the only one who could write my destiny. I really appreciated all of the advice they shared with me.

However, what really shook me to my core is that God starting speaking to me in dreams and visions about things before it actually took place. This he did numerous times which literally scared me initially because I was feeling that God wasn't real. He started communicating with me and stating to me that if he wasn't real he would not be aware of things happening before it's time.

Next, his communications began telling me that the reason I was saying that he was not real was because I was looking to man to be my God. But when I found out that man wasn't real, I said God wasn't real. He showed me that he was with me all along even in my darkest hour. Through all the abuse and pain I suffered, he was there. He showed me that he wanted to use me as a testimony to tell somebody that no matter what they're going through, there is still a God that sits high but looks low on his little children.

The Bible says in (2 Corinthians 3:17), "Now the Lord is that Spirit: and where the spirit of the Lord is, there is liberty." So remember, if there is no liberty in your organization, group or church, there is no God. The Bible says in (1 John 4:8), "He that loveth not knoweth not God; for God is love." Eventually, I decided to go on with my life with the help of Jesus Christ.

My faith was renewed in God. He has shown me in miraculous ways that he loves me and he cares. I was travelling along the expressway one day with my friend, Sylvia. We looked up into the sky and immediately saw a cloud in the form of praying angel. What a sight it was! It was very serene and something we had never in our lives seen before. We perceived this moment as a spiritual connection with God and the praying angel was symbolic as our guardian and protector from hurt, harm, or danger.

My mission now is to warn those who may be involved in a cult, but aren't aware of it; to watch for the signs that I have mentioned in this book. Never sit under the leadership of anyone who wants you to see him as God. See if the person is demanding more and more control of your life. Put God first before any man while there is still a chance. The Bible says that God is love and not abuse (Luke 3:14), "Do violence to no man."

(1 John 4:1), "Beloved, believe not every spirit, but try the spirits whether they are of God: because many false prophets are gone out into the world."

I later divorced my wife, gained custody of all 9 of my children, remarried, continued my ministry, and finally found the right to life, liberty, and the pursuit of happiness.

I hope that my experiences can help others recognize bondage and free themselves before they become the next victims.

Shortly after this book was written in October of 2013, the controversial cult leader, Reverend Arthur Allen fell to his demise and died in a house fire. (Philippians 3:18-19), "For many walk, of whom I have told you often, and now tell you even weeping, that they are the enemies of the cross of Christ. Whose end is destruction, whose God is their belly, and whose glory is in their shame, who mind earthly things."

Characteristics of Cults

Compare these patterns with the situation in which you, a family member, or friend may be involved. This list may help you determine if you are in danger.

This is not intended to be a "cult scale" or a definitive checklist to determine if a group is a cult. This checklist can be used as an analytical tool.

•Questioning and doubt are discouraged or even punished.

•The congregation claims a special, exalted status for itself, its leader, and its members. For example, the leader is considered a messiah, God, a special being or the group and/or the leader is on a special mission to save human kind.

•The congregation has an "us versus them" mentality, which may cause conflict with the society that is not part of the church.

•The congregation teaches that there is justification for whatever acts or behaviors one might convey. This may result in members' participating in behaviors or activities they would have considered shabby or unjust before joining the group. Some examples include lying to friends, family or collecting money for fraudulent charities.

•The leader does not truly respect authorities, teachers, military commanders, or ministers, priests, monks, and rabbis of mainstream religious denominations.

•The leader coax feelings of shame and guilt in order to control members. This is often done through forms of persuasion.

•Submissiveness and vulnerability to the leader or congregation requires them to cut ties with family and friends and fundamentally change the personal goals and activities they had before joining the church.

•The congregation is obsessively concerned in enlisting new members and making money.

•Members are expected to spend an enormous amount of time toward group-related activities.

•Members are encouraged or required to live and socialize only with other church members.

•The leader determines how members must think, act, and feel. Members must get permission to date, marry, buy land, and change jobs.

•The leader dictates the type of clothes to put on, whether or not to have children, how to discipline children, where to live, and how to handle day to day affairs on your job and at home.

•Mind-transformation practices such as meditation, chanting, speaking in tongues, criticizing and ridicule sessions, and exhausting work routines are used massively to suppress doubt about the group and the leader.

•The most loyal members feel that there can be no life outside the group. They believe there is no other way to live and fear, sickness, torment or death will arise to themselves and/or others if they leave, or even consider leaving the church.